I am a JEW

I am a JEW

Clive Lawton
meets
Ilana Goldman

Photography: Chris Fairclough

FRANKLIN WATTS
LONDON • SYDNEY

Ilana Goldman is ten years old. She and her family are Jews. They live in Kenton, which is just outside London. Her father, Herschel, is a civil servant. Her mother, Evelyn, sells Jewish books from a little shop that she runs in their home. Ilana has one brother, Adam, who is twelve.

Contents

This edition 2001

Franklin Watts
96 Leonard Street
London EC2A 4XD

Franklin Watts Australia
56 O'Riordan Street
Alexandria, Sydney, NSW 2015

ISBN 0 7496 4173 8

Text Editor: Brenda Clarke
Design: Peter Benoist
Illustration: Tony Payne

Printed in Hong Kong

The publishers would like to thank the Goldman family and all other people shown in this book.

10 9 8 7 6 5 4 3 2 1

Being Jewish

I was born a Jew so I cannot remember when I first thought about it. But there are many special occasions in the year that remind me of my religion.

Although there are some converts to the Jewish religion most Jews are born into the Jewish people. It is like a very big family. Each year there are many customs and traditions that teach Jews about their history and beliefs.

We have many chances to give presents which remind us to look after other people.

The Jewish religion is a family and community religion so the home and the Jewish community centre, the synagogue, are both very important. All the time, Jews try to remember God and make even ordinary things, like food, special. To show respect to God Jewish men cover their heads, particularly when saying prayers. The little hat that many of them wear is called a kipa.

Shabbat – the special day

Every week our special day, Shabbat, starts on Friday evening when mother lights the candles.

Shabbat starts at sunset every Friday. It is a day of joy and rest. To show that this is a bright and festive day, candles are always lit by the mother. She thanks God when she lights them and covers her eyes as she says a prayer.

After mother has lit the candles, father gives us a blessing from the Bible.

The same blessing was given in the Temple at Jerusalem 2000 years ago. It asks God to look after everybody and bless them with peace. The Jewish Bible is the same as the Old Testament used by Christians.

We use our best things for the three Shabbat meals. Supper starts with a cup of wine to celebrate our special day. Between courses we sing Shabbat songs.

Drinking a cup of wine is a Jewish way of celebrating. There is a special blessing to thank God for the wine. Shabbat table songs and prayers give thanks for the food.

On Saturday evening, when Shabbat ends, I hold the special candle at Havdalla. Adam always holds the spice box.

Havdalla marks the end of Shabbat. The cup of wine is filled to overflowing, to show that the joy of Shabbat should "spill over" to the new week. The scent of spices is breathed in to try and continue the feeling of Shabbat.

Jewish food laws

One way we remember God is by being careful about our food. For example, when I buy sweets, I make sure that the ingredients are kosher.

The Bible has many rules about food. When food fits all the rules it is called kosher. Some food has a sign on the packet which guarantees that it is kosher. Otherwise, many Jews will check the ingredients on the packet very carefully.

Every festival has something special to eat. For Shabbat we either make our own plaited bread or we buy it from a kosher bakery.

One rule is that food with meat in it must be kept apart from food with milk or dairy products in it. Kosher kitchens have two separate sets of plates, pots and cutlery – one for milk and one for meat foods. Ilana's kitchen even has two sinks. Because of special rules about meat, Jews buy their meat from a kosher butcher. Food which contains animal fats or meat must also be guaranteed kosher.

The synagogue and rabbi

Every Saturday morning we go to our synagogue. My favourite part of the service is when the big scroll is taken out of the Ark and paraded round. My father goes to synagogue every day.

Each synagogue has a rabbi who teaches Jews to live according to Jewish traditions. He also leads the people in looking after the poor, the old and the sick. Any man in the synagogue can lead services.

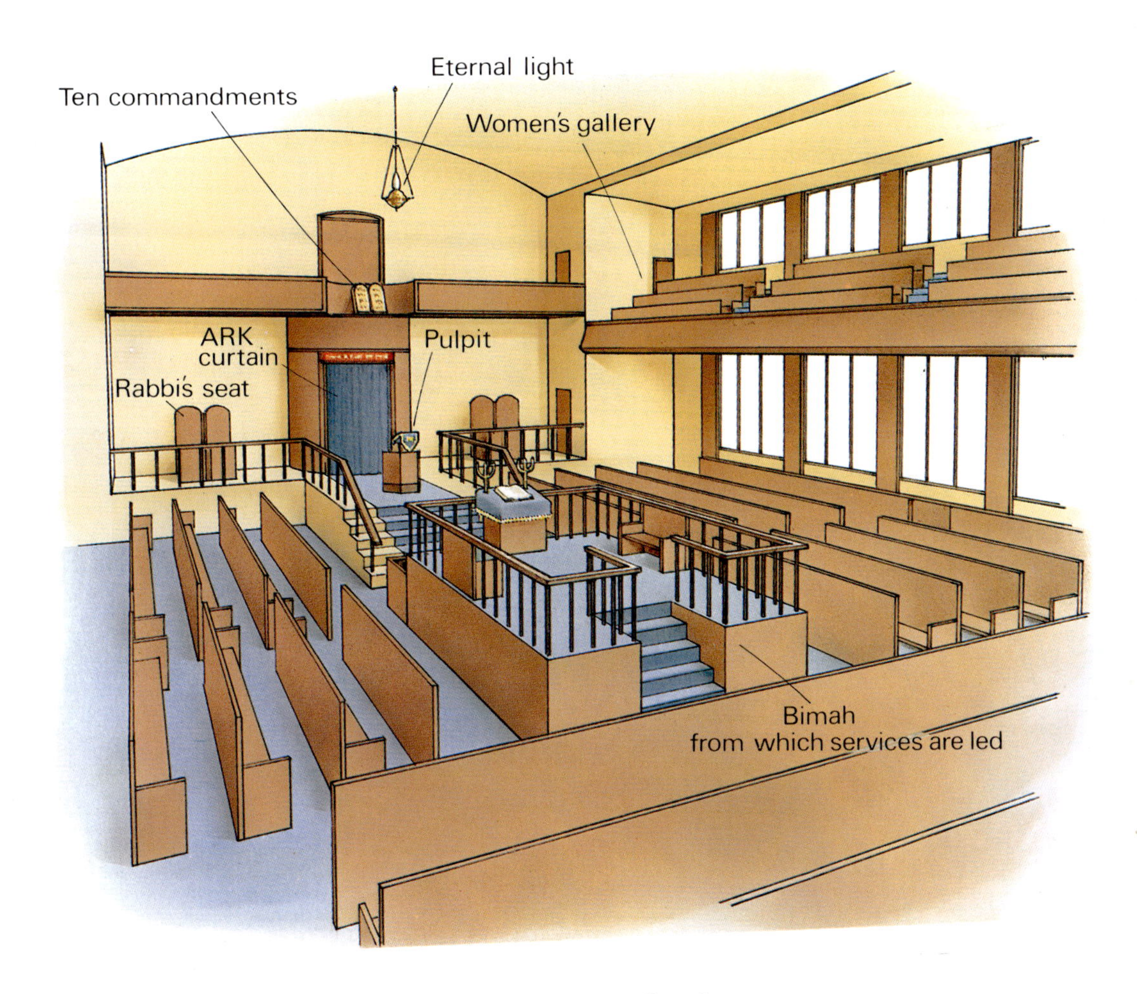

Men and women sit separately in my synagogue. The prayers are led from a platform in the middle. This is called the Bimah.

The picture shows the part of the synagogue in which services are held. A synagogue is also the place where Jewish people gather for meetings and parties. So the building has a hall with a kitchen and classroom.

Learning Jewish customs

On Sunday mornings I go to our synagogue religion school. I also go on Tuesday and Wednesday evenings after school. We learn Hebrew, Jewish history and Bible stories. We make things for the festivals and sing Hebrew songs.

It is important for Jews to know about their traditions. There is a lot to learn – the Hebrew language, 3500 years of history, customs for more than a dozen festivals, the food laws, and all the teachings and stories in the Bible.

Next year my brother is having his Barmitzvah. He has lessons every week to learn how to sing from the scroll of Torah. It takes a scribe about a year to write a scroll.

When a Jewish girl is twelve she has a Batmitzvah. A boy has his Barmitzvah when he is thirteen. Now they are expected to be responsible for their actions and to follow the rules and customs of Jewish life. No longer can they claim they are "only children".

Hebrew

The Hebrew alphabet has only 22 letters and no vowels. Five letters are written differently if they come at the end of a word (inside box). Hebrew is written from right to left so if this were a Hebrew book it would start at the other end. Hebrew is the language in which the Bible was first written. It is also the language of Israel today.

V	H	D	G	B	Silent
ו	ה	ד	ג	ב	א

L	KH	Y	T	KH	Z
ל	כ	י	ט	ח	ז

P/F	Silent	S	N	M
פ	ע	ס	נ	מ

T	S/SH	R	K	TZ
ת	ש	ר	ק	צ

TZ	P/F	N	M	KH
ץ	ף	ן	ם	ך

Shalom שלום

Herschel and Evelyn's family history

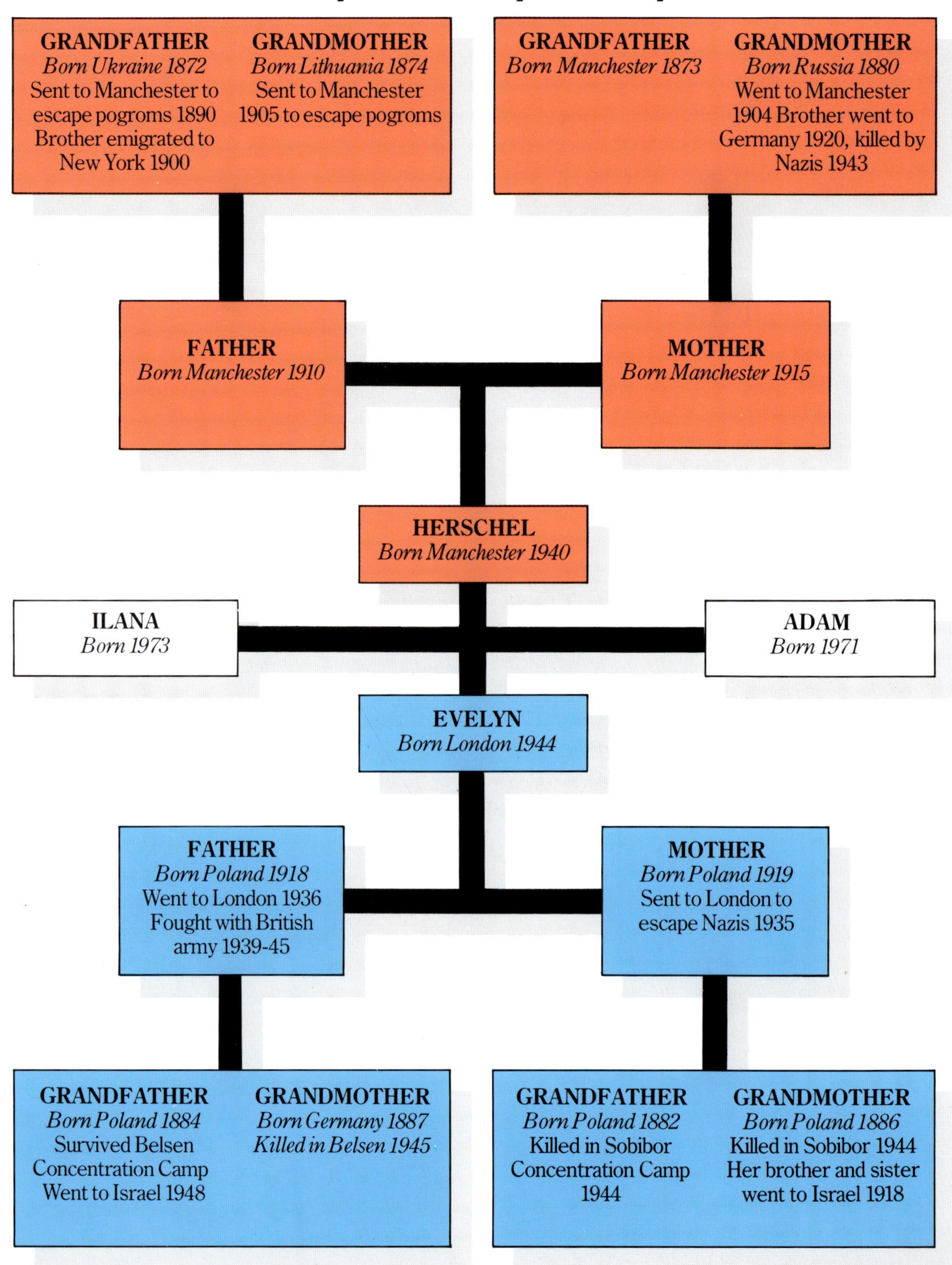

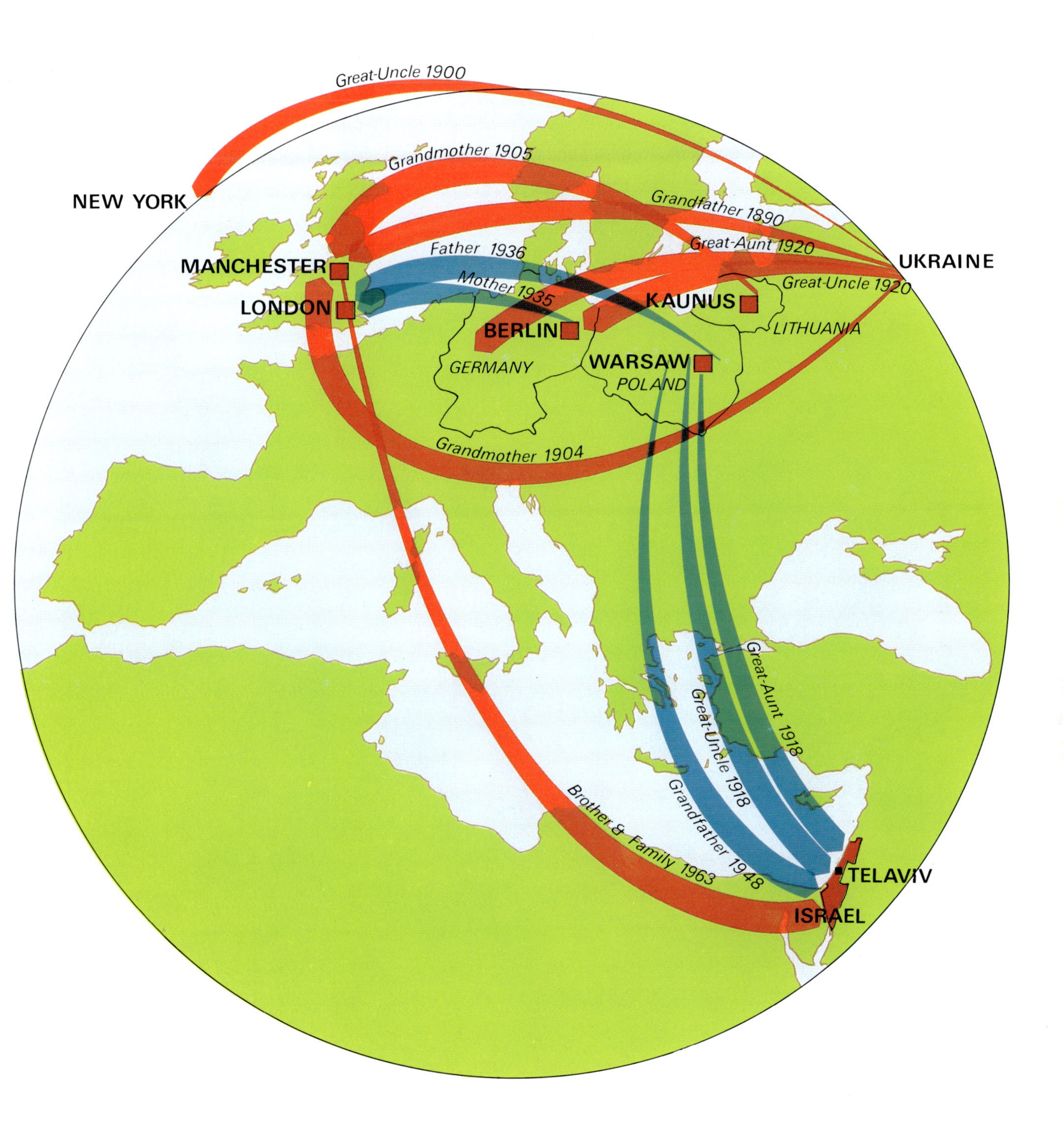

Great-Uncle 1900
NEW YORK
Grandmother 1905
Grandfather 1890
Great-Aunt 1920
UKRAINE
MANCHESTER
Father 1936
Mother 1935
Great-Uncle 1920
LONDON
KAUNUS
BERLIN
LITHUANIA
GERMANY
WARSAW
POLAND
Grandmother 1904
Great-Aunt 1918
Great-Uncle 1918
Grandfather 1948
Brother & Family 1963
TELAVIV
ISRAEL

Passover – the festival of freedom

All the family comes to us for the Seder meal at Passover. Because I am the youngest, I ask the four questions that begin the service.

Passover comes at spring-time. The house is cleaned and all the family gathers for Seder at supper-time on the first evening of Passover. It reminds Jews of the Exodus from slavery in Egypt 3500 years ago. There is a service with questions, stories, games and songs.

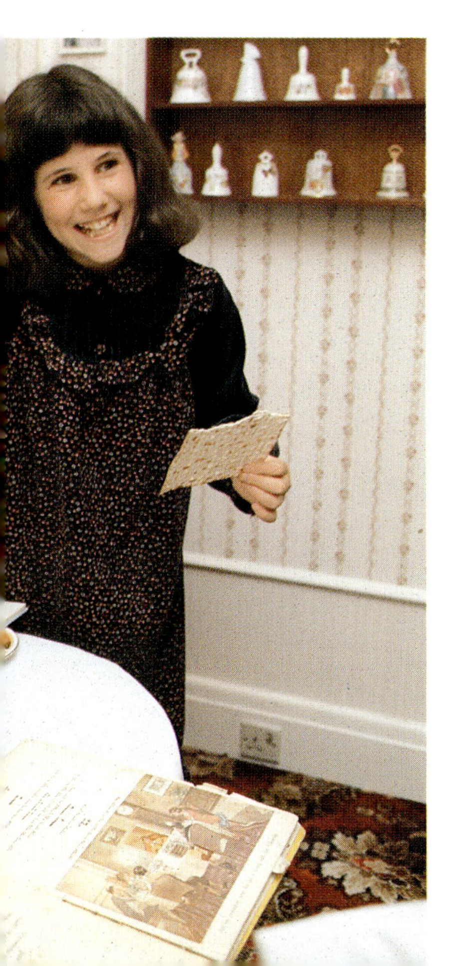

For Seder, we have all sorts of foods that go on a special plate in the middle of the table. After supper, we must find the piece of matza hidden by my father before the service can go on.

Among the foods eaten at Seder are bitter herbs, to remind Jews of their misery as slaves in Egypt all those thousands of years ago. There is also a flat bread called matza. This reminds Jews that in their hurry to escape, they had no time to leave the bread to rise.

Sukkot – the harvest festival

We make our Sukka by taking the roof off our garden shed. We cover the shed in leaves and branches and decorate it with fruit and pictures.

The week-long festival of Sukkot comes in the autumn. The Sukka is a shelter. It reminds Jews that their ancestors lived in tents as they wandered in the desert on their escape from Egypt to Israel.

During the week of Sukkot we eat all our meals in the Sukka, unless it is raining. Without the shed roof, the Sukka is open to the sky!

Every synagogue builds a Sukka for the whole community every year. Families who have enough space in their back garden often build their own Sukka there. In Israel, many flats are specially planned so that a Sukka can be put up on the balcony. Fruit is hung in the Sukka because Sukkot is a harvest festival.

Some other festivals

On Simhat Torah, we take out all the scrolls from the Ark and dance around with them. The children carry flags or toy scrolls.

Simhat Torah comes straight after Sukkot. It means "the celebrating of the Torah". Everybody goes to the synagogue. They dance and sing to celebrate having the special way of life taught in the Torah. Sometimes streamers and sweets are thrown to the children as they dance.

On Hanukka, I light my own candles. The festival lasts eight days, and on each night I light an extra candle. We play the dredle game with a spinning top and give presents to friends and family.

Hanukka is a winter festival. It celebrates the Jews winning back their Temple at Jerusalem about 2100 years ago. The story tells that the oil used for the Temple lamp had nearly all been destroyed. The little oil left lasted eight days, giving the Jews time to make more. The dredle carries Hebrew letters saying "A great miracle happened there".

Purim – carnival time

On Purim, the story of Esther in the Bible is read out. We all have rattles. When the name of "Haman" is said we make such a noise that it cannot be heard.

Purim comes at the end of winter. It celebrates the time when Queen Esther saved the Jews of Persia from being killed by Haman. At this happy festival the synagogue has a carnival feeling.

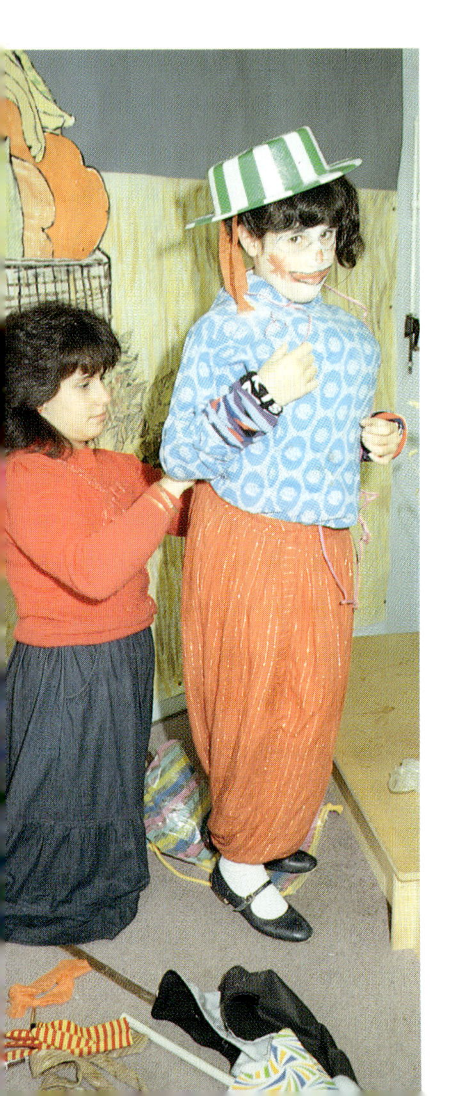

We have fancy dress parties, act plays and take plates of sweets, fruit and biscuits to friends and family.

Purim is a time for all sorts of funny shows and plays. Some people even go to the synagogue in fancy dress. This is another festival for giving presents, especially to people who are too old or too ill to leave their homes. Jews are commanded to see that everybody can join in their happy celebrations.

The Jewish Year

The Jewish calendar is lunar, which means that the months start with each new moon. Each month is only 29 or 30 days long so the whole year has only about 355 days. Seven times every 19 years a whole extra month is added, so a leap year has 13 months.

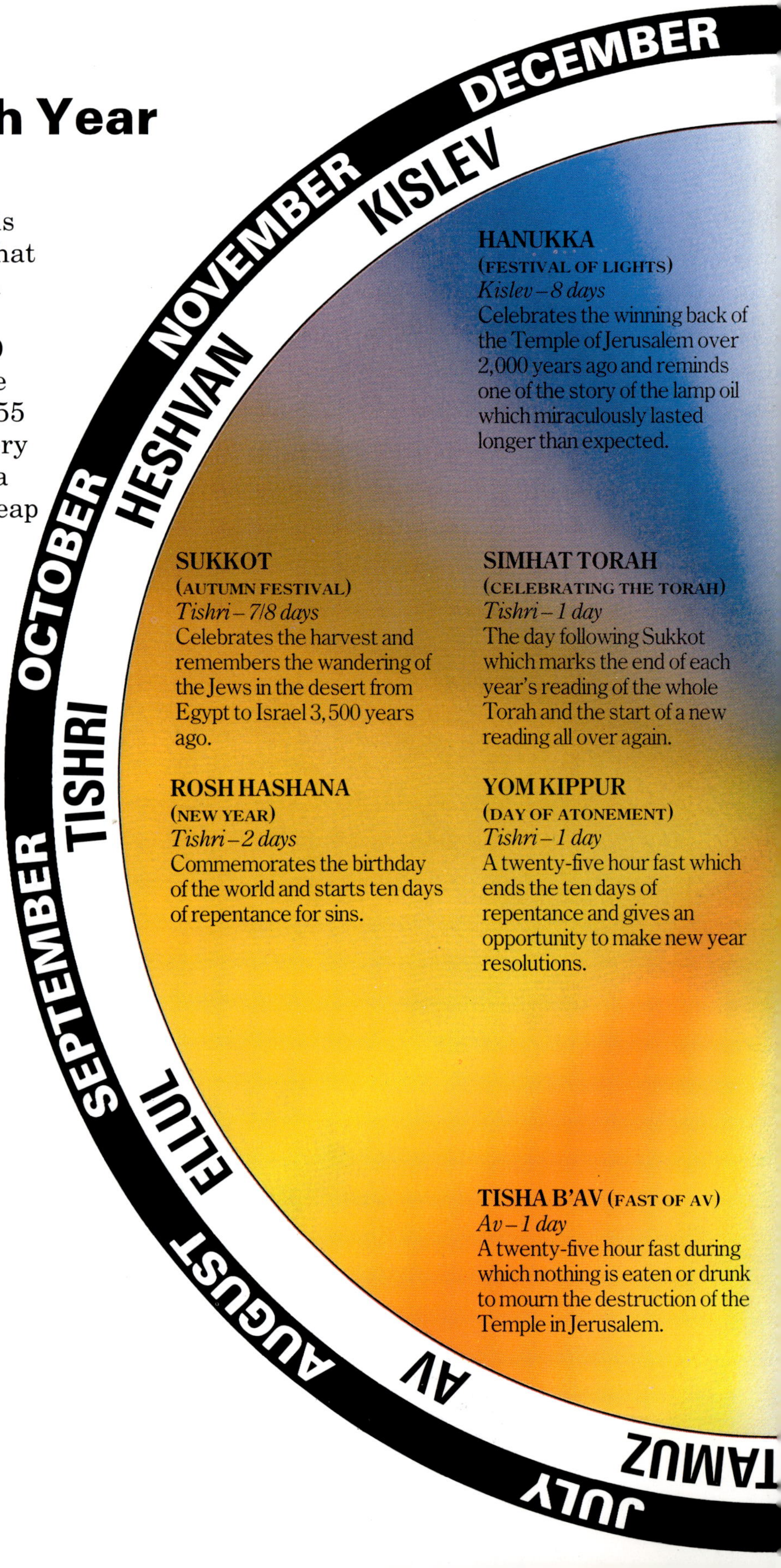

DECEMBER
KISLEV
NOVEMBER
HESHVAN
OCTOBER
TISHRI
SEPTEMBER
ELLUL
AUGUST
AV
JULY
TAMUZ

HANUKKA
(FESTIVAL OF LIGHTS)
Kislev – 8 days
Celebrates the winning back of the Temple of Jerusalem over 2,000 years ago and reminds one of the story of the lamp oil which miraculously lasted longer than expected.

SUKKOT
(AUTUMN FESTIVAL)
Tishri – 7/8 days
Celebrates the harvest and remembers the wandering of the Jews in the desert from Egypt to Israel 3,500 years ago.

SIMHAT TORAH
(CELEBRATING THE TORAH)
Tishri – 1 day
The day following Sukkot which marks the end of each year's reading of the whole Torah and the start of a new reading all over again.

ROSH HASHANA
(NEW YEAR)
Tishri – 2 days
Commemorates the birthday of the world and starts ten days of repentance for sins.

YOM KIPPUR
(DAY OF ATONEMENT)
Tishri – 1 day
A twenty-five hour fast which ends the ten days of repentance and gives an opportunity to make new year resolutions.

TISHA B'AV (FAST OF AV)
Av – 1 day
A twenty-five hour fast during which nothing is eaten or drunk to mourn the destruction of the Temple in Jerusalem.

JANUARY
TEVET
SHEVAT
FEBRUARY

TU B'SHEVAT
(NEW YEAR FOR TREES)
Shevat – 1 day
Trees are planted and everybody tries to eat fifteen different kinds of fruit from trees on that day.

ADAR
MARCH

PURIM
(THE CARNIVAL FESTIVAL)
Adar – 1 day
Celebrates the foiling of the wicked Haman's plan to destroy the Jews in Persia 2,500 years ago, as told in the book of Esther in the Bible.

NISAN

PESACH (PASSOVER)
Nisan – 7/8 days
Celebrates the escape from slavery in Egypt 3,500 years ago and the start of the journey to the Promised Land.

APRIL
IYAR

YOM HA'ATZMAUT
Iyar – 1 day
Independence Day. Celebrates the founding of the State of Israel in 1948.

MAY
SIVAN

SHAVUOT (PENTECOST)
Sivan – 1/2 days
Comes exactly seven weeks after Passover and celebrates the giving of the Torah at Mount Sinai.

JUNE

Jewish Facts and Figures

Only about 355,000 Jews live in Britain. Of these, two-thirds live in London and the rest in about 80 other towns and cities.

There are 14 million Jews in the whole world (not much more than the population of Tokyo, Japan).

About a quarter of the Jews in the world live in Israel.

Over a third of the Jews in the world live in the United States of America. Nearly 2 million live in New York.

Jews are found in about 120 countries of the world. There are Chinese, Indians and black African Jews.

Israel is about the same size as Wales.

The Jews are an ancient people with a history stretching back over 3500 years. Most Jews are born into a Jewish family, but some are converted to the Jewish religion.

Jews do not try to convert people to Judaism. They prefer others to follow their own religious traditions properly.

Israel is the country of the Jewish People. The modern state was founded in 1948.

The history of the Jewish people began in Israel. Jews still face towards its capital city – Jerusalem – when praying.

The first Jew was Abraham, whose story is told in the Bible. Other famous Jews in the Bible are Joseph, Moses, King David, King Solomon, Elijah, Isaiah and Samson.

Jews believe in one God. They try to live according to the teachings laid down in the Jewish Bible.

The Old Testament of the Christian holy book – the Bible – is the same as the Jewish holy book. So this is often called the Jewish Bible. It was originally written in Hebrew so it is sometimes called the Hebrew Bible.

The first five books of the Jewish Bible are called the Torah. This gives the basis of Jewish teaching and tells the story of the beginning of the world and the Jewish people.

The Jewish day begins and ends at sunset.

Jewish law forbids the eating of certain foods including pork and shellfish.

Glossary

Ark The place in the synagogue where the scrolls of the Torah are kept.

Batmitzvah, Barmitzvah Words used to describe a girl or boy coming of age at 12 or 13.

Concentration camp A most cruel form of prison. People are crowded together with little care for whether they live or die. 6,000,000 Jews were killed in the camps set up by the Nazis in the Second World War.

Dredle A little spinning top.

Kibbutz A sort of village in Israel. People on a kibbutz often live by farming. Everybody shares what they have, including the money they earn.

Kosher Anything that fits Jewish law. It is mostly used about food, but can describe anything else. A Sukka without an open roof is not a kosher Sukka.

Matza A flat cracker made of flour and water, but no yeast. This "unleavened" bread does not rise.

Pogrom Riots which took place in Eastern Europe against Jewish communities.

Rabbi A Jewish teacher. Rabbis study for many years. They can have any sort of job, not just that of a teacher or community leader.

Seder The meal and service on the first evening of Passover. It recalls and acts out the story of the Jews' escape from slavery in Egypt 3500 years ago.

Shabbat The Jewish day of rest and celebration. It starts on Friday at sunset and ends on Saturday evening. The Christian holy day, Sunday, is also named after it.

Sukka A hut put up for a short time. The hut has a leafy roof built for the festival of Sukkot in the autumn.

Synagogue The Jewish community centre. Here daily services are held, children are taught and other events take place.

The Temple The Temple in Jerusalem was the central place of worship for Jews. It was built by King Solomon about 2700 years ago and destroyed by the Romans 800 years later. The building has gone, but part of the Western Wall still stands.

Index